The Water Cycle

by David Smith

Illustrations by John Yates

Wayland

Titles in the series

The Human Cycle
The Food Cycle
The Plant Cycle
The Water Cycle

Words printed in **bold** can be found in the glossary on page 30.

First published in 1993 by
Wayland (Publishers) Ltd
61 Western Road, Hove
East Sussex BN3 1JD

British Library Cataloguing in Publication Data

Smith, David
  Water Cycle. – (Natural Cycles Series)
I. Title II. Yates, John III. Series
333.91

ISBN 0 7502 0693 4 **Hardback**
ISBN 0 7502 1412 0 **Paperback**

Series Editor: Kathryn Smith
Series Designers: Robert Wheeler and Loraine Hayes
Artwork: John Yates

Typeset by: DJS Fotoset Ltd, Brighton
Printed and bound in Italy by Canale.

Contents

Water everywhere

If you were an astronaut gazing down on Earth, the first thing you would notice is that most of the Earth's surface is covered with water. In fact, water covers nearly three-quarters of our world's surface.

The next time you pour yourself a glass of water, watch carefully how the water moves. Water is a **liquid**. It can flow and take on the shape of any object that holds it.

Water can change. If it is cooled down it will freeze and turn into ice. Ice is a **solid**. We can make ice in a freezer. Look at some ice cubes. Can they flow like water? Do they have their own shape?

ABOVE The blue area on this special photo is the Pacific Ocean. Look how much of the Earth's surface it covers!

When water freezes, it turns into ice crystals. They can form beautiful lace-like patterns.

Most of the world's ice is found at the South Pole (Antarctica) and the North Pole (the Arctic). Some ice is also found at the top of very high mountains where it is very cold.

If ice is warmed up, it will melt. When water is warmed up it will change into **water vapour**. Water vapour is a **gas**. Gases can spread out in all directions. You can see this happen when a kettle boils. Watch what happens to the steam. Water vapour is all around us in the air.

Some of the water at the North and South Poles is frozen in huge icebergs, like this. They may contain ice which has been frozen for thousands of years.

Fresh water, salty water

Like many other creatures, these fish must live in salt water to survive.

1% Fresh water

2% Ice

97% Salt water

Imagine this glass of water contains all the world's water. This shows just how little fresh water there is.

Most of the world's water is **salty** and is found in seas and oceans. Some plants and creatures need this salty water to survive, so they can only live in the sea.

This tree frog needs to keep its skin wet with fresh water to stay alive.

The water in our ponds, lakes and rivers is called **fresh** water. Many plants and animals live in fresh water. Others need it to drink, just like we do. In fact, humans use more fresh water than any other animal.

Humans use huge amounts of fresh water everyday, in all sorts of ways. Even swimming pools are filled with fresh water.

Only a tiny part of the world's water is fresh water that we can use. It seems amazing that we have never run out!

The reason why there always seems to be enough is that nature recycles fresh water. This has been going on ever since water was first formed over 4 billion years ago. This recycling is called the **water cycle**.

Disappearing water

The water cycle starts in the open seas. The Sun shines down on the sea water, causing some of it to evaporate.

Our journey round the water cycle starts in the open seas. As the Sun shines down on to the sea, the heat from the Sun turns some of the water into tiny drops of water vapour. The water vapour rises into the sky, carried upwards by warm air. This process is called **evaporation**.

This part of the water cycle is very important. When sea water is evaporated, all the salt in it is left behind in the sea. This means that the water is pure and fresh.

See for yourself

See for yourself how salt water evaporates in the Sun, leaving salt behind.

You will need; table salt, a plastic saucer or dish and a marker pen.

1. Fill the plastic saucer with a mixture of fresh water and 2 teaspoons of salt. Then mark the level of the water in the dish.

2. Place the saucer on a window ledge in a sunny position. Mark the water level each day.

3. What happens to the salt water eventually?

Evaporation does not just happen over the sea. It can happen anywhere where there is water and sunshine. In sunny weather, rain puddles soon dry out. Even ponds and lakes dry up a little, because of evaporation. Water also evaporates from plants and trees.

When wet washing is hung out to dry, the water evaporates into the air.

Gathering clouds

As warm air carries the water vapour higher into the sky, it cools down. Cold air cannot hold as much water vapour as warm air. So eventually the water vapour turns back into liquid water. This change from water vapour to liquid water is called **condensation**. You can see this happening, when water vapour in the air condenses on a cold window pane.

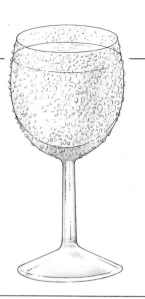

The air is full of tiny **particles** of dust. When condensation happens, millions of tiny drops of water are made around the dust, making clouds.

If you look at the skies, you will see many different patterns of clouds. All these different patterns come from three main types of cloud; cirrus, cumulus and stratus.

Cirrus clouds are thin and wispy. They are made of ice crystals and are found high above the Earth's surface, where the air is very cold.

Note the wispy appearance of these cirrus clouds.

The stratus clouds in this picture look like thick fog. Compare them to the fluffy cumulus clouds.

Stratus clouds can be seen in layers or sheets across the sky. They are found at lower levels above the Earth than cirrus clouds. Stratus clouds often blot out the Sun and the blue sky, bringing rain or drizzle.

Cumulus clouds look like fluffy bits of cotton wool. They have flat bottoms and are often seen dotted around the sky on sunny days.

Cloudburst

Inside a cloud, water drops bump into each other and join together to make larger drops. The larger drops grow too heavy for the cloud to hold on to, and they fall down to Earth as rain.

It begins to rain when larger water drops in clouds grow too heavy for the cloud to hold on to.

Rain is only one of the ways in which the water cycle brings water back to the surface of the Earth. Water may also fall as hail and snow. Hailstones are raindrops that have moved back up into a freezing cloud on rising **air currents**. The raindrops freeze into solid balls of ice and then fall as hail. Sometimes the hailstones can rise up and down inside the cloud many times before falling. Each time they rise into the cloud, another layer of ice is added and they grow larger. The largest hailstone ever measured landed in Kansas in the USA, in 1970. It was 19 cm across. Thankfully most hailstones are no bigger than a pea!

How rain is made

Raindrops start as tiny drops of water vapour.

Bigger drops are made as the smaller ones join together.

Cross section of a hailstone

By slicing a hailstone in half and counting the layers of ice, a weather scientist can tell how many times the hailstone has risen back into the cloud.

How snowflakes are made

Snowflakes start as tiny wafers of ice.

The ice crystals attract each other and join together to make beautiful snowflakes.

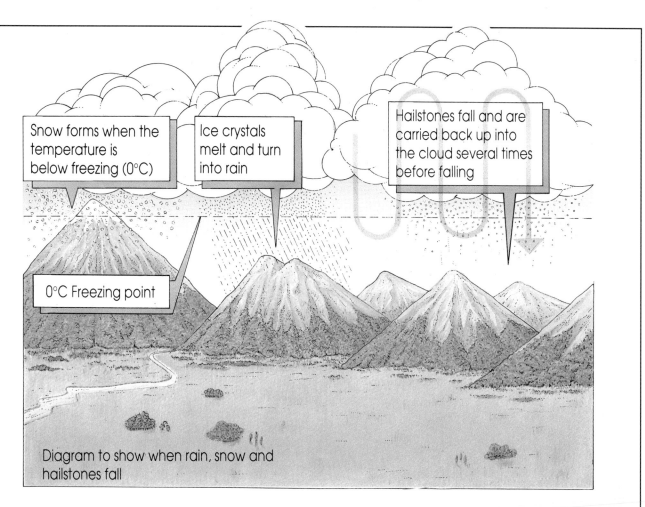

Snow forms when the temperature is below freezing (0°C)

Ice crystals melt and turn into rain

Hailstones fall and are carried back up into the cloud several times before falling

0°C Freezing point

Diagram to show when rain, snow and hailstones fall

Snow falls from clouds that are made of ice crystals. Inside these clouds, the ice crystals grow into snowflakes by joining to other crystals. Then, as long as the air temperature below the clouds is cold enough, the snowflakes fall to Earth. Often the temperature below the clouds is warmer and the snowflakes melt and turn to rain. If the snowflakes fall in a very cold place they never melt. The snow is pressed down into ice and stays there for thousands of years.

The delicate pattern of a snowflake is made when ice crystals join together.

Filling the rivers

When water has fallen as rain, snow or hail, it continues its journey by running back into the rivers. This is the next step along the water cycle. Water can find its way back into the rivers in many ways.

Rain-water seeps into the soil and rock

Plants and trees drink up rain-water

Rain stored in reservoirs

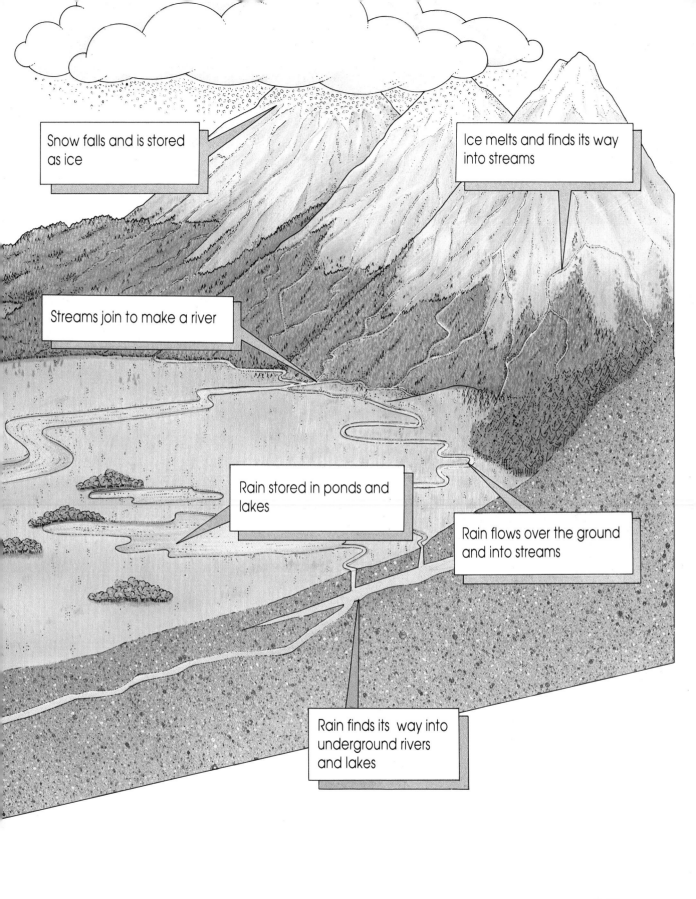

Snow falls and is stored as ice

Ice melts and finds its way into streams

Streams join to make a river

Rain stored in ponds and lakes

Rain flows over the ground and into streams

Rain finds its way into underground rivers and lakes

A supply of fresh water

Have you ever stopped to think just how easy it is for us to turn on the tap when we want fresh water?

The fresh water in our rivers can be used in many different ways. Some water is taken out of our rivers and stored in **reservoirs**. Reservoirs are huge lakes that have been made to hold water. This water can be pumped to factories where it is used to cool down and clean machinery.

Fresh water is also pumped into our homes, schools, shops and public buildings. We use this water for drinking, washing and cooking, so it has to be very clean. For this reason the water is **treated** before it reaches our taps. Leaves and dirt are removed by **filtering** the water through gravel beds. **Chlorine** is added to kill any harmful germs. The people treating the water then make sure that it does not contain any dangerous **chemicals**.

When the water is clean and safe enough for us to use, it is pumped through underground pipes to where it is needed.

Farmers need a supply of fresh water for their animals to drink and to help their crops grow. It is not as important for this water to be treated, so farmers often take it straight from rivers, ponds or underground wells.

This water channel in France catches rain-water. Farmers use it to water their crops and animals can drink from it.

Water treatment

Dirty water is called **sewage**. Sewage travels in large underground pipes called sewers to the sewage works where it can be cleaned.

When water has been used, it is dirty. Think of all the ways you use water everyday.

First the sewage passes through a large tank where any big bits of grit are removed. Next it is moved into a settling tank. The sewage stays here until all the tiny bits in it have settled to the bottom of the tank to make a **sludge**. The liquid sewage at the top of the settling tank is piped over a filter bed. Here, air is bubbled through the sewage to help **bacteria** grow. The bacteria attack and get rid of any germs and dangerous waste. Then the sewage is filtered through fine pebbles to take out any remaining bits.

The clean water that is produced by the treatment is called **effluent**. The effluent is now clean and safe enough to go back into our rivers and continue its journey along the water cycle.

Gravel filter beds in a sewage plant are used to help clean dirty water.

See for yourself

See for yourself how to clean dirty water. You will need; muddy water, filter paper, some gravel, some sand, some charcoal powder and a plastic bottle.

1. Cut the top off a plastic bottle, turn it upside down and rest it on the remaining part of the bottle.
2. Place the filter paper inside the bottle top and fill it with a layer of the wet sand.
3. Pour the muddy water on to the sand.
4. Watch carefully as the water drips through. What do you notice?

Can you improve your filter, using the gravel, sand and charcoal powder?

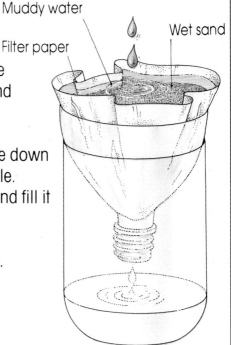

Muddy water
Wet sand
Filter paper

Water pollution

This picture, taken under a microscope, shows the tiny creatures that live in all fresh water. Would you like to drink water with these in?

In the natural **environment**, water is never as clean as when it comes out of the tap in our homes. It is alive with tiny plants and animals. Look at this picture on the left of clear mountain stream water. It was taken under a **microscope**. It shows that fresh water contains many tiny living creatures which we cannot see with our eyes. Without these tiny living things, the larger plants and animals in our ponds and rivers would be unable to survive.

But this water is not fit for humans to drink. So, if natural water is already dirty, what is water **pollution**?

Pollution is anything harmful in the water that nature did not put there. Pollution often harms plants and animals, and sometimes kills them.

Rubbish dumped thoughtlessly into ponds and streams looks ugly and can be dangerous. Waste water from farms, houses and factories is sometimes not cleaned properly. It may take chemicals and sewage back into the rivers and lakes from which it was taken.

This poor bird is covered in oil. When oil is spilled in our seas, wildlife always suffers.

This kind of pollution can cause terrible damage to the environment.

Many chemicals that are useful to us are also harmful **pollutants**. The chemicals in washing-up liquid do a great job on dirty dishes, but what happens when they get into the water cycle?

Dumping rubbish in a pond not only looks ugly — it causes terrible damage to the plants and animals that live in it.

See for yourself

See for yourself how washing-up liquid pollutes fresh water. You will need; a tray of water, a paper clip and some washing-up liquid.

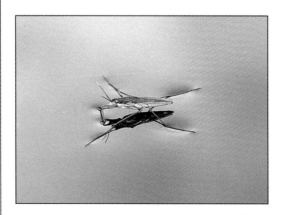

1. Place one paper clip carefully on the surface of the water so that it floats.

2. Now add a drop or two of washing-up liquid. What happens? Can you find out why?

How might pollution by these chemicals affect the pond skater in this picture?

A pond skater stands on the surface of the water.

Return to the sea

Cleaned and treated water returns to our rivers. All rivers eventually reach the sea, and the water in them finally completes the water cycle.

A river's journey starts high up in the mountains. The river starts life as a small, fast-moving stream which tumbles down the steep slopes of hills and mountains. At this stage the water in a mountain stream looks crystal-clear.

Diagram to show a river's journey, from high up in the mountains down to the sea.

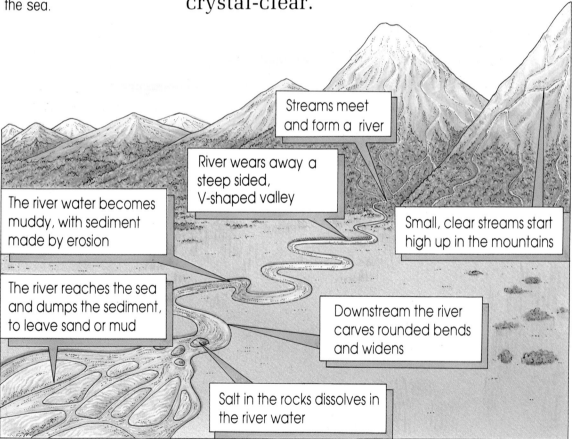

Streams meet and form a river

River wears away a steep sided, V-shaped valley

The river water becomes muddy, with sediment made by erosion

Small, clear streams start high up in the mountains

The river reaches the sea and dumps the sediment, to leave sand or mud

Downstream the river carves rounded bends and widens

Salt in the rocks dissolves in the river water

Mountain streams join together and widen in to a river.

The river carves itself a valley out of the land as it flows towards the sea. Rivers make their valleys by **erosion**. The power of the water carries stones and rocks along the river bed. These stones and rocks scrape away at the river bed and eat into the banks. As the river flows to the sea, it gets wider and deeper. The water is now much more muddy than it was. This is because it is full of tiny particles made by erosion.

As the river flows over rock, it **dissolves** the salt in the rock. The amount of salt in the fresh river water is tiny but it is carried out to sea. When the sea water is evaporated, the salt is left behind in the sea and the water cycle starts again.

TOP A river begins life high up in the mountains, as a tumbling stream.

BELOW A river widens and deepens as it flows towards the sea.

Fast and slow cycles

Rainforests get over 2000 mm of rain each year. In Britain the city of London receives 550 mm each year.

Tropical rainforests, found near the **equator**, have the fastest water cycle in the world. In these areas the whole water cycle happens in just one day.

It is always very hot in rainforests. The heat causes a lot of water from plants in the forest to evaporate into the air. The warm air holds a lot of water vapour. But eventually so much

evaporation takes place that the air cannot hold any more water. When this happens a short, violent rainfall takes place.

Hot deserts have the slowest water cycle in the world. Sometimes, it can take years before it rains in a hot desert.

The air over deserts is hot and dry during the day. It does not rise up and cool down, but keeps close to the ground, staying hot. Any water vapour in the air during the day cannot condense and form rain clouds. This lack of rainfall in a desert is called a drought.

Deserts receive very little rain each year. Some years they receive no rain at all. Most plants and animals find it very difficult to live in deserts.

The Water Cycle

Cooler temperatures cause condensation and clouds to form

The Sun's rays warm the ocean and the land

Water vapour is carried up by rising warm air

Evaporation of water from plants and soil

Evaporation of water from the sea

Evaporation of water from lakes, ponds and rivers

The energy to drive the water cycle comes from the Sun. Water changes from vapour, to liquid, to solid and back to water again. This natural recycling of water is vital to the survival of all life on Earth.

Temperature below freezing

Water turns into ice crystals in freezing temperatures and snow falls

0°C Freezing point

Snow stored as ice

Temperature above freezing

Water droplets do not freeze, but join together to make rain

Ice melts when temperature is above freezing (0°C)

Rain falls, and flows across and under the ground into rivers

Rain-water taken up by plants, trees and animals

Rivers take some of the water out to sea

Glossary

Air currents Flows of air. If warm, they will rise.

Bacteria Tiny germs which are all around us.

Chemicals Substances which, when mixed together, change into something different.

Chlorine A chemical added to water to kill bugs and germs.

Condensation When water vapour changes into liquid water, due to cooling.

Dissolves To melt into something. Salt dissolves in water.

Effluent Water produced after sewage is cleaned.

Environment Everything around us, including our homes, the countryside, towns and buildings.

Equator An imaginary line running around the centre of the Earth.

Erosion The wearing away of the land by water or wind.

Evaporation The changing of water to water vapour, brought about by heating.

Filtering To pass water through sand and gravel to make it cleaner.

Fresh water Water that is not salty.

Gases Air-like substances that take up the whole of the space containing them.

Liquid Anything that can flow, such as water.

Microscope A special machine which allows us to see tiny things which we cannot see with our eyes.

Particles Very small bits.

Pollutant Something which causes pollution.

Pollution Damage to the environment caused by

waste material.

Recycled Something that is treated so it can be used again.

Reservoir A specially-built lake, made to store fresh water for use by humans.

Salty water Water containing salt.

Sewage Waste water from houses and factories.

Sludge A muddy substance that is made after sewage has settled.

Solid Any substance that has its own shape and does not flow. Wood is a solid.

Treated To deal with something, to make it safe.

Tropical rainforests Thick forests found near the equator. They are full of thousands of plants and animals.

Water cycle The natural process that recycles water.

Water vapour The gas into which water is changed by heat.

Further Reading

Weather by Steve Parker (Kingfisher, 1990)
Water by John Baines (Wayland, 1991)
Water by Diane McClymont (MacDonald, 1987)

Picture acknowledgements
The publishers would like to thank the following for allowing their pictures to be reproduced in this book: Bruce Coleman 11 (J. Foott), 12 (top, J. Shaw), 25 (bottom, F. Prenzel); Environmental Picture Library 7 (top, P. Brown), 28 (M. Mckinnon); Zul Mukhida 9; Oxford Scientific Films 6 (L. Gould), 22 (top); Science Photo Library 4 (top, T. Vant Sant), 13 (A. Pasieka), 18 (S. Terry), 21 (M. Bond), 25 (top, Dr M. Read); Tony Stone Worldwide (cover picture, centre and background, bottom), 5, 6 (bottom), 8 (D. Bjorn), 15 (K. Hilsen), 24 (top, G. B. Lewis), 27 (P. Lamberti), Zefa 13, 19, 24, 26 (G. Braasch).

Index